Another Look Back at Lynn
(1945 to 1970)

Dedication

To my brother, Richard Booth (1948 - 2007)

Tricky Sam Publishing

Foreword

At the end of the war times were hard with the country perilously close to bankruptcy. The only thing we had plenty of was community spirit because, in order to succeed, we all had to 'pull' together.

Before the war some people believed that a woman's place was in the home – that all changed when the men folk went off to war. During the war women could be found working everywhere – in factories, on the railway, on farms, as fire fighters and as anti-aircraft gunners.

At the end of the war food was still rationed and, despite less food, we were better (more healthily) fed. Not only food, but also essentials like coal, petrol and clothes were also rationed. To every young boy's delight even soap was rationed! Rationing ended in 1954 when butter and meat were finally de-rationed. The current trend is for recycling, but this is only small scale when, during the war, everything that could be recycled was recycled by necessity (remember 'make do and mend').

After the war workers were entitled to one week's paid holiday – this entitlement had only been introduced in 1939 but was generally postponed owing to the war. Prior to 1939 the only paid holiday was for bank holidays, and there were few complaints.

The new government of 1945 set about nationalizing the railways, electricity, gas, coal industries and the Post Office (which had it's profitable businesses slowly taken away over the ensuing years). Has privatisation made these industries less efficient, too complicated and even more expensive?

The introduction of the credit card was the start of large-scale borrowing and, in the late sixties, one of the banks offered an _unsecured_ personal loan of £100 to _non_-customers. This was the start of the seduction to win customers when lending would escalate to recent levels - in the early 1970s a slogan to encourage borrowing was 'Take the waiting out of wanting'.

Relaxing credit caused high inflation, and while people saw their house value rise dramatically (giving the feeling of being better off) it was all relative. Banks lent more and more to increase their profits and this led to house price inflation leading to today when house prices are beyond the first time buyers. The banks only have themselves to blame for their present predicament.

The situation has now come full circle where, before the war, the majority could only afford to rent.

The figures are purely arbitrary but show the impossible situation today's first time buyers find themselves in:

Year	1945	1960	1970	2008
Approx. cost of a 3 bed semi	£550	£1800	£4100	£150000
Average wage (annual)	£250	£700	£1500	£22000
Cost of house/average wage	2.20	2.57	2.73	6.81

Acknowledgements

John Allen	Diana & Derek Chappell	Paddy Green	Annette McGivern	Henry Souttar
Tony & Ann Allen	Copper Roller Bearings	Gerald Groom	Gary Madge	David Thomas
David Andrews	Doug Crisp	Steve Hammond	Rick Meek	Pat Thorpe
Julie Austin	Beryl Drew	Norman Hastings	Angela Mitchell	Peter Todhunter
Roy Backham	Liz Dyer	Jane Johnson	Pete & Mina Mott	Bill Turner
Keith Boughen	Jack Eagle	Tony Jubey	Maureen Plowright	Bill Wagg
Sheila Broughton	Eric Field	Ann Kerry	Brian & Wendy Rose	June Walker
Ray Bullock	Brian Fisher	Reg Knight	Terry Rose	Gary Wiles
John Bunting	Lynda Fuller	Amanda Lovejoy	Beryl Sleight	
Roger Carter	Colin Fysh	Rene Lusher	Ian Smith	
Sue Carter	Dick Goodchild	Eddie Lyon	Ken & Jill Smith	

Introduction

As with the previous book (Looking Back at Lynn, A Scrapbook of the 50s & 60s) I have tried to follow a chronological theme. Only this time starting with 1945 (the end of the war) and covering the next 25 years to the end of 1969. In 1945 the population of Lynn was about 23,000 and by the end of the 1960s it had risen to about 30,000. It is hard to estimate the population today, but a figure of over 40,000 has been mentioned.

Again the quality of the photographs varies owing to many different sources. I must also stress that, although I have tried to give accurate descriptions, invariably I cannot guarantee the validity of some of these descriptions. For those pedants who buy this book, I'm sure if you look hard enough you will find some inaccuracies, but for the vast majority I hope you will enjoy it for the nostalgia it brings.

This is not meant to be a definitive historical work but a fond look back on our town and, maybe, the pictures will invoke your own (hopefully happy) memories.

The copyright of photographs from the Lynn News, West Norfolk Borough Council and the Eastern Daily Press is acknowledged and gratefully appreciated.
A special thanks to all the staff at the Norfolk County Council Library & Information Service, King's Lynn for all their help to the author, to photographer Brian Fisher who had the foresight to record many of the local scenes used in this book, Colin Bailey of Fraser Dawbarns for his legal expertise, John Allen for proof reading, Wilson & Betts for their continued support and to Janet for her help with layout and cover design.

When time, who steals our years away,
Shall steal our pleasures too,
The memory of our past will stay,
And half our joys renew

The second world war was over in 1945 after six years of extremely hard times, the horror of which, subsequent generations would never appreciate. Celebration was the order of the day when numerous street parties took place. It was all about community spirit, somehow not quite the same today. TOP: Residents of George Street. ABOVE: Dilke Street pose for the cameraman before tucking into a feast (rationed of course), the like of which no-one had tasted since 1939.

LYNN NEWS & ADVERTISER—Friday, May 18

ONE OF LYNN'S VE TEA PARTIE

LYNN NEWS & ADVERTISER
Incorporating LYNN AVDERTISER (Est. 1841). LYNN NEWS (Est. 1860), Etc.

No. 10,278   Tel. 2692   FRIDAY, MAY 11, 1945   Postage 1½d.   Price 2d.

RFOLK CELEBRATES VICTORY IN EUROPE

e Dance—
d Think

BONFIRES

ving Planned
ay

Europe with spontaneous rejoic-
spirit of heartfelt gratitude and

and helpers decked out in red,
te and small, with fireworks of
g people have sung songs, old
danced in the open and under
ckground of flags, bunting,
pre-war Christmas parties and
tea-parties are planned.

official days' holiday. Public-
supplies warranted; they have

Happy faces round a Victory tea-table at St. Ann's Fort, Lynn. Thi
typical of many street tea parties held in the
appear in next T

King Edward VII. school blackout shutters formed the basis of this satisfactory bonfire on the
school field on VE-Day. The Mayor—an old boy—visited the fire and partook of roasted potatoes.

TOP: Regent Street and ABOVE: Gladstone Street party in the summer of 1945.

ABOVE: St. James Infants in 1946. The school was for boys from about five to seven years old (they then usually went to St James Primary school in Hospital Walk). The girls stayed on until age eleven when they would go to secondary school.
Miss G Oliver was headmistress of the Primary Infants' school.

MIDDLE RIGHT: The Convent produce a play in 1946.

BOTTOM RIGHT: Gaywood Primary school, Rosebery Avenue in 1946.
The school was built in 1908, replacing a voluntary school in Gayton Road (which then became the church rooms).

A favourite stopping place to and from the school was Panks sweet shop which had opened in Rosebery Avenue in 1912.

Priory Lane in 1946. The property on the extreme right was originally a pub (The Valiant Sailor) but at this time had been split into two abodes. During the 1950s the celebrated artist Walter Dexter lived in the old pub - which had become one property again. Priory Lane, with its 18th century cottages, contains much of the remains of an early Benedictine Priory. A wide 15th century arch can be seen, which was probably an entrance into the priory. The properties that can be seen at the bottom of the lane in Church Street were virtually all derelict and were demolished in the early 1950s. After school we boys (from St James Boys School) would explore these ruins along with similar ruins in Bridge Street. Luckily the health and safety officer wasn't around in those days!

LEFT:
King Street looking north from the bridge over the Purfleet in 1946.
The end of Purfleet Street can clearly be seen.

There are (surprisingly) quite a few cars parked along here considering the war was only just over – the drivers could park with impunity (the title 'Traffic Warden' had yet to enter our vocabulary!).

The cars were probably owned by accountants & lawyers and their clients as this was where many of the professions had their offices. The Lynn News offices and works were on the right in King Street. The properties on the left of the street were originally merchant's houses.

8

ABOVE: Dolphin Inn 1946. Situated in Friars Street, at the end of Southgate Street, the inn, which closed after Christmas 1907, was by now converted to three houses (or in modern parlance, apartments) - these were vacated in the mid 1955s. The single storey building to the right of the inn was a skittle alley which finished when the inn closed. It was later used to garage cars.

BELOW: By 1960 the property (now empty) has been boarded up. Evidence of a scrap yard is on the wall of the old skittle alley in the right hand picture below.

LEFT:
North End under 18 football team in 1948. Winners of Lynn minor league (1947 - 1948), the Convoy cup & others.

Back row (left to right): Alf Parr, Bill Mendham, Peter Johnson, Tony Whiting, Ivan Lilley, Ray Shirley, Eddie Frost, Harry Frost, Pop Marshall (chairman).

Front row (left to right): Ted Witt, Ken Smith, Laury Wakefield, Albert Balls (club president), Ben Webber, Peter Gadsden, Tony Mist.

RIGHT:
The Labour Club 1948.
The club's snooker team pose in the grounds after winning the Riley Shield.

Back row (left to right): W Hunt, M Masters, P Green (steward), T Little, W Jones, D Skerritt.

Front row (left to right): G Watson, G Fox, D Evetts, G Hunt, T James.

LEFT:
St. James Boys Football team 1947/48.

Back row (left to right): Mr Beaumont, Derek McClennan, Tony Booth, John Guy, Alan Ludkin, Mick Page, Mr Turner.

Front row (left to right); Alan June, Alan Roberts, Gerald Groom (captain), Alan Rake, Terry Gilligan, Terry Greenacre.

The Purfleet (c1947). The Custom House on the right. The large grain silo was built in the late 1930s and is owned by CW Byford & Sons Ltd. (corn merchants). The ship (a steam coaster) is the Stock Force of Whitehaven (built 1917) and is loading grain, most probably to be transported to London. This ship did not dock at the Purfleet silo after 1948.

ABOVE: The Queen opening the new maternity unit at Hospital Walk in 1949.

LEFT: 1946. South Wootton Sunday school outing to Hunstanton.
Back row (left to right): Wendy Gamble, June Gamble, Eileen Drew, Mrs Sims (teacher), June Toll, ? Morrison, Alec Tasker, Sheila Mallett.
Middle row: Roberta Moore, Christine Blood, Margaret Blood.
Front row: ?, Margaret Barnard, ?, Rosemary Sims, Judith Brown, ? Brown.

LEFT: c1947 Stepney Baptist Sunday school outing to Hunstanton. The Stepney Baptist Chapel was built in 1841 and is in Blackfriars Street next to Blackfriars Hall.

THIS PAGE & PART OF THE FOLLOWING PAGE: Gaywood Park Boys 'long' school photograph of 1949.
By now the school had been operating for 10 years having opened on 11th September 1939.

TOP & ABOVE: The right hand end of the Gaywood Park Boys long photo in 1949.

LEFT:
Gaywood Park Boys Football team, winners of the Norfolk Schools Football Association Challenge Shield, 1948/1949.

TOP: Hardwick Road on 10th April 1951 looking east (the road sign in the distance indicates where the A10 and A47 diverge). The field on the right behind the trees is Sillett's cricket pitch - the pavilion can just be seen between the trees. This hut was originally used by the High School on a playing field down Estuary Road. After Campbells bought the site the hut was again moved to South Wootton to continue use as a cricket hut eventually succumbing to developers of a new housing estate in the late 1960s.

MIDDLE: On the same day across the road is the Hardwick Road Filling Station and Café owned by Wilfred Batterham.

BOTTOM LEFT: The road in July 1960 and still little traffic. Two men effect a road repair without all the cones and associated signage we see today!

BOTTOM RIGHT: It's now September 1963 with Campbell's Soups less than five years old, there is still little evidence of traffic. Despite the lack of traffic we still managed to run our lives (get to work, get the weekly shopping , travel etc.) - do we really need to use our cars so much today?

TOP: Tower Street in November 1950. The men staring out of the upstairs of No.8 suggest it is being renovated but the first recollection I have of it being occupied was in about 1954 when it became the Pink Grill café.

BOTTOM: Further up Tower Street 29th July 1959. On the right is Batterbee & Co (pork butchers) and on the left is Barnaby & McLean (paints and wallpaper). A wary old lady watches the 'bubble' car as she attempts to cross the road.

TOP: The Tuesday Market Place (3 acres) in 1950. Up to the 1790s women were burned here at the stake. There was also the pillory and stocks. If the local authority failed to provide the pillory and stocks they forfeited the right to hold a market.
ABOVE RIGHT: The Dukes Head in 1962 [originally the Griffin or Gryffyn Inn] was rebuilt from an earlier hotel in 1685 by Henry Bell (who was the architect of the Custom House). In 1948 you could have a double room for 25/- ('*ration books must be produced*').

ABOVE LEFT: The Maids Head in August 1959. During the sixties this became a mecca for pop music - frequented by many well-known pop groups of the time thanks to the owners Colin & Mary Atkinson.

RIGHT: The staff of the Dukes Head enjoy themselves at a staff party in 1964. It was really a very special occasion to have a meal in the dining room - the first time I remember coming here was in the late 60s for Janet's 21st. Sunday lunches were very popular and could attract 100 plus customers even in the early 90s.

TOP: The staff of Ely's (William Ely & Sons) of Norfolk Street. Ely's was a well known bakers and restaurant at 4, Norfolk Street. The staff held their annual dinner at the Town Hall, seen here in 1950.

BOTTOM: c1951/2. The girls of St. James Primary Girls' school (Paxton Terrace) pose for the camera. Behind is Railway Terrace. Miss G Watts was headmistress of the Primary Girls' school.

Top row (left to right): Wendy Fox, Doreen White, Maureen Bowman, Beryl Hudson, Valerie Howlett, ?, Maureen Chapman, Maris Peake, Angela Courtman.

Second row: Bunty Foster, Jill Dixon, ?, Jennifer Sayles, Maxine Manning-Coe, Ann Golden, Myra Crack, Pat Pygall, ?, ?, ?

Third row: Rosalyn Finney, Gwendoline Uttin, Margaret Leverett, ?, Goolie Smith, Diane Rastell, Margaret Howell, Carol Trigg, ?, ?, Muriel Farrow, Prunella Bensley

Front row: Margaret Baldock, Diane Pearce, Sylvia Fisher, Ann Pattingale, Vivienne Tinkler, Maureen Savage, ?, ?, Vivienne Skate, ?, Margaret Smith, Ann Petts

THESE girls who, on leaving home for Lynn High School, on Wednesday expected nothing more exciting than their usual lessons, but found they had unexpected visitors in the Queen and Princess Margaret. With the Queen is Mr. J. H. Catleugh, chairman of the School Governors.

As seen in the Lynn News (1951)

FROM TOP LEFT CLOCKWISE: High above the shoppers and traffic in High Street, Mr A Bird gives a coat of bright aluminium paint to a lamp standard, one of the many in the town which are undergoing their periodic clean-up. He is working on one of the wrought iron ornamental arches with the Lynn coat of arms at each side. The Queen visits the High School. In June the girls of Gaywood Park cheer their team on during the Lynn Schools' Athletic Association Secondary Schools' sports on the boys school ground. The girls of the High School perform JM Barrie's comedy 'Quality Street'. The girls are *(left to right)* Janet Sauvain, Jenny Kiddell, Rosemary Patterson, Patricia Paterson and Ruby Barnes. Derek Low and Bernard Tyrell of the 12th troop do some 'mangling' during Bob-a-Job week. Members of the Lynn Model Railway club (Valingers Road) survey their handiwork. Inset left is Bernard Latus and Doris Willis (the only female member) operating the switchboard control panel. Ron Winter (second left in the main picture) is the club leader.

TOP: London Road by the South
Gates in 1950, showing the entrance
to Southgate Street. On the left of
the photo is The Honest Lawyer.

MIDDLE: The junction of Windsor
Road (on the right), Goodwin's
Road (on the left), Guanock Terrace
ahead (leading to London Road) and
Windsor Terrace.

BOTTOM: The corner of Windsor
Road and Windsor Terrace. Mrs EM
Willimott's (fruiterer) shop is open.
Sometime in the mid 1950s this
became J Bone's greengrocers.

TOP: Gaywood Park Girls - 3A1 are the PT winners in 1950.

RIGHT: 1950, Highgate School (built 1878). Crossing the road are Paddy Mears, Victoria Valentine, Irene Smith and Gillian Day. For many of us this was our first school. My first teacher (who served many years here) was Miss Fysh. In the late 1940s we were bussed to the Stanley Buildings in St James Road for lunch. The buildings had been built in 1883 and housed a library previously. I will always remember this school with great affection.

BELOW: Easter 1951. Gaywood Park Boys, Townshend House.

TOP: The staff of the Hospital, in football fancy dress, enjoy a Christmas party in 1950. It is only two years since the formation of the NHS - this year (2008) it celebrates it's 60th anniversary. I would like to pay a tribute to all the hard working staff at our hospital who always put our well-being first despite the impossible workloads they have. I have witnessed staff who frequently put in more (unpaid) hours to see their jobs through rather than 'knock off' at the end of their shift - and still be fully attentive to patient's needs.

MIDDLE LEFT: The staff of Ladyman's enjoy a conga in the Dukes Head ballroom in 1950.

MIDDLE RIGHT: The Snettisham Hillbillies (aka Luke Harrison and his Hillbillies) perform at the Grosvenor in January 1952.

BELOW RIGHT: A square dance for children was taking place with the help of the Hillbillies. The picture of the band was published in The Lynn News, who wrote *'Pupils of Mrs E R Myers, the Lynn music teacher, enjoyed square dancing at their party at the Grosvenor Restaurant, Lynn'*. Here they are seen trying their hand at the new dance craze.

TOP: King's Lynn Reserve team. Winners of the Peterborough league cup & invitation cup 1950/51.

Back row (left to right): Eddie Griffiths (trainer), Ron Isbell, Ken Smith, Matt Evans, Eric Hodge (ex Spurs), Wally Price (ex Tranmere), Alf Kimber, Jack Gardner (team manager).

Front row (left to right): Jock Hutton, Neville Norman, George Rumbold (ex Ipswich), George Heagren, Len Adams.

BOTTOM: King's Lynn Cricket Club, July 5th 1950. The team and their opponents (Norfolk County Club & Ground CC) are photographed before the opening match at Gayton Road. At the end of the war Norman Boughen founded Newlyn CC with friends in the area. This became King's Lynn Cricket Club - Mr Boughen being captain until 1954.

Back row (left to right): ?, CRS Boswell, ?, ?, ?, KS Hubbard, W Watson. *Second row*: EC Harcourt, L Rowe, GH Whitmore, A Clarke, ?, W Bridges, ?, GAR Moore, A Smith. *Third row*: H Hendrie, D Green, Alderman Catleugh, WS Thompson, N Boughen, Mr Gauvain, JA Eagle, W Younge. *Front row*: ?, M Franklin, HL Grant, ?, A Burgess.

23

TOP: Plowright, Pratt and Harbage, 7 & 8, Norfolk Street (Ironmongers), decorated in 1952 to commemorate Queen Elizabeth's accession to the throne. The company was opened in 1822 by Henry Plowright and closed in 1992.

BOTTOM: Plowright, Pratt and Harbage (usually referred to as just 'Plowrights') hold a staff party at Christmas 1959.

TOP: Reliance Motor Engineers (& cars for hire) in Valingers Road in 1954, looking towards All Saints Street.
BOTTOM: A view of the bottom of Valingers Road looking in the direction toward London Road. The photographer is standing at the junction with South Lynn Plain and Friars Street (on the right). The building on the extreme left is the Anchor pub.

TOP: King's Lynn School of Commerce annual prize giving at the Tower Restaurant in New Conduit Street on Saturday 7th November 1953. This was run by Murdins of St. James Street. The man in the bow tie on the front row was Mr Bradshaw (the owner of Murdins), on his left was Freda Easton (teacher) and on her left was Mrs Bradshaw.

ABOVE: King's Lynn Ladies Choir entertain in the interval of the BBC broadcasted Brains Trust in the Corn Exchange in 1954. The chairman of the Trust was well known broadcaster Macdonald Hobley. The mayor & mayoress, Mr & Mrs Bernard Bremner attended the entertainment. One of the choir members won a 180 guinea television set - this would have been some prize bearing in mind that the average weekly wage was around £7 in 1954. For those not familiar with the currency of the day, a guinea was 21/- or £1.05.

I wonder how the calculator generation would manage with our old non-decimal currency, length, weight etc.?

RIGHT: 1952. Four Convent girls pose in their distinctive uniform in the grounds of the school in Goodwins Road.
From left to right: Jennifer Larrington, Carol Varney, Ann Green, Sheila Mallett.

TOP: The Guildhall, Christmas 1958. Sinbad The Sailor at the Arts Centre. Sinbad was played by June Robinson, the Princess by Wendy Ashwood and the Dame by Clem Prescott. Also featured was well known magician Graham Wilson. On the extreme right the old man of the sea was Eddie Lyon who later produced very many shows.

MIDDLE: The Royal Borough School of Dancing (run by Miss Phyllis Pickering) put on a performance of Me and My Teddy Bear in 1952. The dancing school was based at 27, Railway Road.

RIGHT: In 1955 cubs of the 15th Gaywood pack and their leader, Mrs Sheldrake, admire their award of first prize in a Road Safety Competition. It had been presented to them by the Mayor, Mr Walton, at the Town Hall.

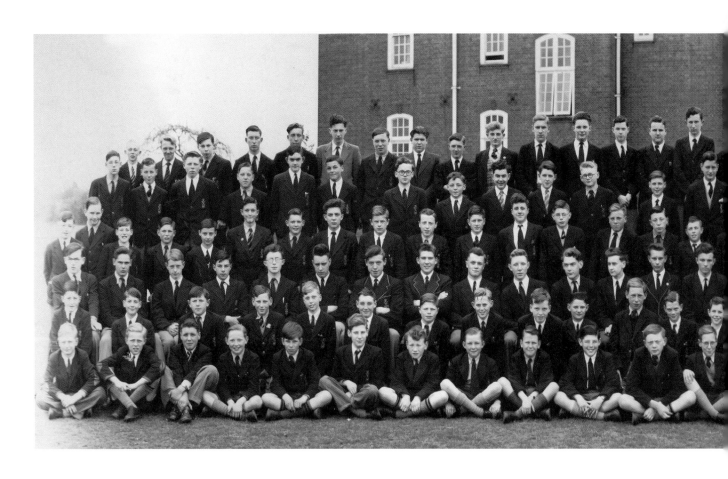

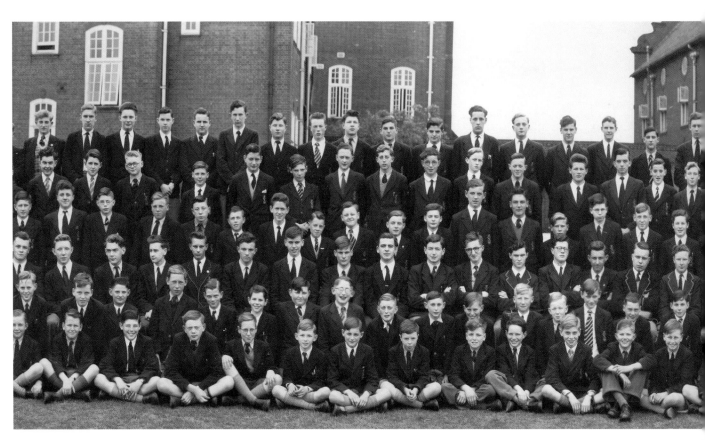

Over this and the next page is a 'long' school photograph of the Grammar School (KES) from 1954. The building in these first two sections was the boarding house. At this time there were about 40 boarders whose parents either worked abroad or whose families lived too far away to travel by day. The area in front of the boarding house was out of bounds to day boys - to trespass would mean detention, such was the severity of school rules. Very few dare break the school rules as punishment would be detention, the cane or expulsion and school boys and girls respected the discipline of the day.

TOP: KES sports day 1955. Ian Bachelor heads for the tape in the senior 440 yards. Members of staff scrutinize the climax of the race. Holding the tape is Mr Staden, behind him wearing a flat cap is Mr Rowe, behind him (standing on a chair) is Mr Freestone (who had been mayor in 1953) and on the extreme right is Mr Vernon.

BOTTOM: KES sports day 1966. Gary Wiles takes a mighty leap to break the junior school long jump record by over a foot - this record stood for over 30 years. His record for the intermediate long jump (18ft 10in) in 1968 still stands today - 40 years on! Behind the trees is the Hunstanton railway line and the houses are in Hulton Road.

LEFT: No.8 Chapel Lane in June 1956. This, the last house in the lane, was (and still is) known as the Exorcist House.

The other seven houses were demolished in the sixties.

BELOW LEFT: A view of the rear of the house from St Nicholas church yard.

RIGHT: A view looking down the lane from Austin Street - just round the corner is the start of Pilot Street. My grand parents lived at No.6 and I have spent many happy hours here, watching my grandad and his brother turning out all sorts of engineering pieces of equipment from his shed in the back yard. Between them they devised a winch system for most of the shrimp boats, which made landing a haul easy by using the boat's engine. Grandad's nephew, well known fisherman Frank Castleton, wrote in his excellent book 'Fisher's End' that:

'The winch was built mostly from parts of the original twenties T Ford engines and that some were still working in the late 1980s. For many years it was a godsend to the local fishermen.'

Round the corner in Pilot Street my aunt Flo kept a sweet shop - paradise!

31

TOP LEFT: Summer outside the Baths in the mid 50s friends sit chatting - life was certainly never boring. *Left to right*: Janet Preston, Mary Williams, David Reed, Christine Proctor, ?, Paddy Mears.

TOP RIGHT: Prefects of Gaywood Park Boys c1954.

LEFT: A well known ballerina appears at Gaywood Park Girls in 1956 to give a display to the girls.

RIGHT: A group of 'Tec' students wait outside the King's Lynn YMCA in St. James Street in the mid 50s. This building was originally the Lynn Savings Bank, erected in 1858.

The college had out-grown the building in Hospital Walk so classrooms were found in many locations in town. About four rooms were used here along with rooms at St James Club further along the street. There were also rooms adjoining the old Tower Restaurant in New Conduit Street and Park Annexe in St James Park. Until the new college in Tennyson Avenue became fully operational in the mid 60s I would spend a lot of time driving from one location to another to teach various classes - surprisingly the students never complained if I was late!

TOP: The junction of Chapel Street and Norfolk Street in August 1956. From the right of the picture the shops are: A Hutson (sewing machines), Arthur Clarke (butcher) in his last year of trading, Laidlow's (furniture), Edward Towler (hairdressers) and nd Chain Libraries Ltd. Across the street is The Grosvenor and Fiddamans.

ABOVE: The end of Norfolk Street - between Kirby Street and Blackfriars Road in 1956. From the right of the picture is Trixies wool store) and another branch of Laidlow's. I think the shop next door is about to become RAP (rented radio) Ltd.

ABOVE: London Road (South) Methodist Chapel choir in 1955. The chapel was opposite Bowskill's (chemists) and was demolished in the 1960s.

MIDDLE LEFT: 1956. Fifth formers pose outside the Tuck Shop at the Grammar School in 1956. This was run by a Miss Lane and provided sweets, current buns, sausage rolls, lemonade and, my favourite at the time, Wagon Wheels.

LEFT: Gaywood Park Boys cricket first X1 in 1956.

Back row (left to right): Trevor Hawes, Graham Skipper, ?Rippon, ?Ashling, ?, ?.

Front row: Barry Smith, Keith Brookes, Malcolm Nichols, Reg Turner, Roger Stokes.
Front (sitting): Stanley Ward, ?.

TOP: Class DS1 of Gaywood Park Girls proudly show off their Christmas cakes in 1957.

BOTTOM: Gaywood Park Girls prefects visit Mr & Mrs Catleugh at home (The Grange) off Wootton Road on their 50th wedding anniversary with headmistress Miss Bullock in 1958.

TOP: The local train for Hunstanton has just left Lynn station in 1958. The man on his trade bike has come from Tennyson Avenue and is heading for the footbridge over the line into Gaywood Park. The bridge over the line had been built in 1941 - this would save Gaywood Park school pupils coming from town and South Lynn a long walk round to reach the school.

BOTTOM: The train having arrived from Liverpool Street now departs for Hunstanton - the locomotive is a more powerful engine than the usual motive power for the Hunstanton branch. The two white discs indicate that this is an express passenger train. Meanwhile a goods engine awaits its turn of duty - again in 1958.

The box below the single signal indicates the platform number to drivers of arriving trains.

TOP: A goods train makes its way from the docks to the station in the late 1950s. The driver and firemen would have signed on at the loco shed and then biked to the docks to take over from the early shift, hence the transporting of the bikes on the front of the engine. In the background is the Pilot cinema.

ABOVE: A view of the dock line from Pilot Street (in the 1960s) looking towards the station. Unfortunately this track has recently been removed so that any chance of moving imports and exports by rail is now impossible. In view of the increasing amount of traffic on the roads round Lynn, I think this may be rather short-sighted.

LEFT: Shunting takes place on the dock line adjacent to Dodman's in the mid 1950s.
The photo has been taken from Dodman's bridge.

TOP: St. James Street in 1962. The wall on the right of the photo is part of St. James Club (St. James House) and home of King's Lynn Conservative Club (and also used by the County Technical College to provide extra classrooms).

BOTTOM: In 1958 the Watch Shop on the corner of Church Street and Norfolk Street receives the attention of a sign writer. Opposite is the White Hart Stores pub.

RIGHT: The 1957 ladies annual Ouse swim. Some of the swimmers pose for the cameraman beside the South Quay watched by a large crowd - they will be rowed across the river to start the race from West Lynn.
Left to right: Heather White, Margaret Simpson, Pat Webber, Christine Proctor and Paddy Mears.

BELOW LEFT: The end of the race - waiting to be pulled from the water.
BELOW RIGHT: Gaywood Park Girls team receive a briefing from Beryl Coates (the sports teacher) at the King's Lynn Quad sports in 1956.

BOTTOM: Gaywood Park Boys Athletics team in 1959.

Back row (left to right): ? Turner, Roger Oliver, Maurice Bunton, John Cork, Dudley Empson.
Front row: Pat Smith, Terry Rose, Rodney Howlett, Larry Seaman (sports master), Keith Ashwood, Robert Hudson, 'Dumper' Bilham.

39

ABOVE: Church Street in 1959. A lot of the derelict properties have now been demolished but Johnson's Motor Works remains.

LEFT: Tower Place in February 1959. This shows the sheer size of WH Johnson's. It occupied most of the land bounded by St. James Street, Tower Place, Church Street and Stonegate Street.

BELOW LEFT: The main showrooms on the corner of Tower Place and St James Street in February 1959.

BELOW RIGHT: This picture was taken at Johnson's in 1947. The Lynn News printed the picture with a story about the three men having served Johnson's for over 100 years between them. The man on the left is Fred Petts, the man in the middle is my granddad (also Bob Booth) and on the right is his brother (Bill). My granddad, like most people of his generation, hardly ever had a holiday since paid holidays were non-existent before the war.

TOP LEFT: High Street looking south on 6th May 1959. TOP RIGHT: High Street looking north the same date. Millers had taken over Murdoch's where I bought my first record in 1954 (78rpm of course!).

BOTTOM: Another view of High Street looking north at the same time. On the right of the picture is the Queen's Head, and next door is the East Anglian Trustee Savings Bank. The Hovis sign is above Woodcocks (bakers & restaurant). On the left is Westons (costumiers), the next shop is currently empty, then Roses (sports), the hanging sign belongs to Curry's (cycles, radio & television).

TOP: Gaywood Park Girls Staff 1959
Back: Miss Hargreave, Mrs Ely, Mrs Richardson, Miss Draper, Miss Beeby, Miss Lane, Miss Ballantyne.
Middle: Mrs Gwynne, Mrs Williams, Miss Coates, Miss Blatherwick, Mrs Gittens, Miss Dunwoody, Mrs Morrison, Miss Snelling.
Front: Mrs Reynolds, Mrs Robinson, Miss Williams (Deputy Head), Miss Bullock (Head), Miss Freeman, Mrs Catton, Miss Brown

BOTTOM : King Edward V11 staff c1960
Back: Mr Taylor, Mr Smith, Mr Greenwood, Mr Upcher, Mr Bayfield, Mr McCall, Mr Trist, ?, Mr Perry
Middle: Mr Hood, Mr Stittle, Mr Hales, Mr Middleton, Mr Gregory, Mr Thornton, Mr Meek, ?, Mr Reason.
Front: Mr Price, Mr Williams, Mr Grant, Mr Hatton, Mr Sleigh, Mr Beaumont, Mr Vernon, Mr Gwynne, Mr Fisk.

Another 'long' school photograph of the High School taken in the courtyard in 1959. These first two sections are of the left-hand
nd.

TOP: The right hand end of the 1959 High School long photo.
BELOW: KES Civic students visit the Houses of Parliament in 1957, seen here with the local MP Mr Scott Miller (on left).

Students: *From the left*: Laurence Bliss, David Rice, John Bell, Barry Britton, Fred Noble, Geoffrey Ashton, Gordon Parnell, David Jameson, Michael Boon, John Bunting, John Allen, Michael Webb and Mr RF Stittle (teacher).

TOP: Norfolk Street looking east in 1959. Chilvers is on the corner at the junction with Austin Street and the Duke of Edinburgh pub is on the corner at the junction with Blackfriars Road, beyond is Littleport Street. BOTTOM LEFT: Further along, another shot of Norfolk Street looking east. BOTTOM RIGHT: Opposite Catleughs at this point is an alley leading to Harry Boltons (antiques), seen here in the late 60s. Before 1965 this building had been George Oswells' (printers).

TOP: South Lynn station in August 1952. A holiday excursion has arrived (09.35 from Nottingham) at 12.17, en route to Yarmouth Beach (due to arrive at 14.53). The Nottingham engine pulls away from the train as the fireman of the Yarmouth engine (which had worked a train to South Lynn from Yarmouth in the morning) affixes the excursion number (M64) before coupling to the train in order to continue the journey eastwards (to leave at 12.30). This 10 coach train had no buffet - passengers had just 13 minutes to refresh themselves in the station buffet! There would be another chance to take refreshments when the train reached Melton Constable but the passengers would only have 8 minutes there as the train then ran non-stop to Yarmouth!

BOTTOM: South Lynn, 14th February 1959 - only two weeks left before closure of the M&GN system, a local train (the 1.40 pm for Peterborough North) departs and heads west across the Ouse (at roughly the same spot as the current bypass) to Sutton Bridge and thence on to Peterborough. In fact the A17 to Sutton Bridge follows the old track bed of the line.

TOP: Gaywood Park Girls perform a concert for refugees in 1959 (World Refugee Year).

ABOVE LEFT: Gaywood Park Girls enjoy their school Christmas party in 1959.

ABOVE RIGHT: Jermyns at Christmas 1959. Maureen Dennis (left) with little Julie Austin, who has decided she'd rather hold on to her doll than sit on Father Christmas' knee. Of course she would have no choice today!

TOP: St James Street in 1955. Bensley's (radio and TV) is No. St James Street and Stokeley's (tobacconists) is No. 10. These two shops are currently occupied by 'The Record Shop' - probably the biggest in Eastern England for collectors of vinyl records and second-hand CDs.

BOTTOM: The top of Tower Street in 1959, at the junction with St James Street. On the left is the Rummer Hotel and, on the right, Wheelers TV and ahead is Tower Place leading to the Millfleet - the shop that can be seen on the 'Fleet' is R&K Tann (general store). To the right of that shop is the passage that leads to Coronation Square (which was actually more of a triangle than a square).

TOWER STREET 1950	TOWER STREET 1970
From Baxter's Plain to St. James' Street	**From Baxter's Plain to St. James' Street**
North-east side	*North-east side*
1 Edward Wm. Thos. florist	1 Dryden & Son watchmakers & jewellers
3 Dryden (Lynn) Ltd. watch makers	3 Dryden & Son watchmakers & jewellers
here is South Clough lane	**here is South Clough lane**
5 Berry Mrs E E gowns	5 Loades Peter Ltd, domestic appliance dealers
7 Modern Book Shop	7 Book & Toyshop, booksellers
9 Stone Miss Florence, tobacconist	9 Seaman T A tobacconist
11 Charity Geo. baker	11 Phoenix Chinese Restaurant
here is Leach's Yard	Brien H, French polisher (**Leach's Yard**)
13 Brown B. & Sons, fruiterer	13 Baby land, baby linen
15 Barnaby H C fishmonger	15 East Anglian Trustee Savings Bank
17 Bambridge's, fruiterer	17 East Anglian Trustee Savings Bank
19 Goodson Wm. fishmonger	19 East Anglian Trustee Savings Bank
21 Barnaby & McLean, wallpaper merchants	21 McLean C Ltd wallpapers & paints
23 Loades Peter, radio engineer	23 Bush W. R. fish caterer
25 Loades Peter, radio engineer	25 Bush W. R. fish caterer
27 Bush Jsph. fish caterer	27 Bush W. R. fish caterer
29 Neal Sidney Wltr	29 Neal Mrs D M
31 Medwell Miss Mabel baby linen	31 Medwell Miss Mabel baby linen
Methodist Church School Hall	Kings Lynn Youth Centre
33/39 Watts & Rowe, printers	33/39 Watts & Rowe commercial printers,
Rummer Hotel	Rummer Hotel
South-west side	*South-west side*
Majestic Cinema	Majestic Cinema / Majestic Dance Studio
4 Golden Ball P.H.	4 Norwich Building Society
6 Bayes Chas radio engineer	6 Bayes Recordium (record dealers)
8	8 Terra Nova, furniture boutique
10 Starling Mrs D I	10 Pets' Paradise, pet shop
12 Hill Miss Alice, tobacconist	12 Teene Boutique
14 Ruhms Geo Edwd hairdresser	14 Ruhms Geo Edwd hairdresser
here is Union Lane	**here is Union Lane**
16 Verry H & Son, sports outfitters	16 Money's, sports outfitters
18 Watsons', picture frame makers	18 Lilians, ladies' outfitters
	18a Hendry & Co. (Builders) Ltd
20 Batterbee & Co pork butchers	20 Batterbee & Co. pork butchers
22 Lancaster Wm A pork butcher	22 Kennedy Anne, ladies' hairdresser
24 Isles J R wool shop	24 Isles G R wool shop
26	26 Zoo. animal dealer
28 Bullen E R grocer	28 Model Shop (S. Morris), toy dealer
Brooker Jn Ltd. Motor engineers	
Tower Roller Skating Rink	King William H. Ltd used car centre
30 Isles Geo	30
32 Wittred Fredk. Hy. tobacconist	32
34 Wittred Fredk. Hy	34
36 Cresey Chas. Rt. boot maker	36
38 Spinks Alfd. confectioner	38 Wheelers television dealers

Although these two streets were secondary shopping streets they were both part of the town's shopping circuit until the Millfleet bus-station moved to a more central position in the early 1970s. Shoppers coming by bus from the north and east of the town tended to alight at Townsend's corner and finish up either back at the corner or the Millfleet. Shoppers from the south and west would alight at the Millfleet and then return there on their way home. After the mid 1970s when the bus station moved from the Millfleet to the town centre these two streets became less popular with shoppers, although specialist retailers still attract custom.

ST JAMES' STREET 1950	ST JAMES' STREET 1970
From Saturday Market place to London Road *South side* **here is Church Street**	**From Saturday Market place to London Road** *South side* **here is Church Street**
2a Rees Wm E watch maker	
2 Pratt & Coldham, hairdressers	2 Pratt & King, hairdressers
4 Errington Et. Geo. tailor	4 Court Bros Ltd. House furnishers
6 Westwood Misses, confectioners	6
8 Bowers Geo. butcher	8
10 Stokeley Et. tobacconist	10 Bensleys Ltd electrical appliances
12 Bensleys of Gaywood Ltd. Cycle dealers	12 Bensleys Ltd electrical appliances
14 Three Pigeons PH Alfd. E	14 Westminster Wine, wine & spirits
16 Wilson E. & Son Ltd. furriers	16 Greeves Mrs W
16 Greeves Jas. Wm. painter	16 Co-operative Permanent Building Society
18 Johnson W H & Sons Ltd. Motor engineers	18 Prudential Assurance Co. Ltd
20 Eastern Gas Board	20 Snow White Coin Operated Laundry
22 Taylor Ed. Ernest, fruiterer	22 Taylor R E fruiterer
24 Johnson W H & Sons Ltd (offices)	24 Jones J Ltd (house furnishers)
26 Audrey Madame ladies' hairdresser	26 Audrey Madame ladies' hairdresser
28 Bennell F W & Son, bakers	28 Prime J. bookseller
30 Sawyer A G butcher	30 Sawyer A G butcher
36 Johnson W H & Sons Ltd. Motor engineers	36 Mann Egerton (Johnsons) Ltd.
here is Tower Place	**here is Tower Place**
Theatre Royal	Theatre Royal
here are Tower Gardens & London Road	**here are Tower Gardens & London Road**
North side	*North side*
1 White Hart Stores P.H.	1 White Hart P.H
5 County Electrical Services Ltd. Electrical engineers	5
7 King's Lynn YMCA	7 YMCA
9 & 11 Peak H W Ltd. house furnishers	9 & 11 Court Bros. Ltd (house furnishers)
13 St James' House / St James' Club	13a King Wallace Ltd. House furnishers
13 King's Lynn & West Norfolk Conservative Club	13b Carters, radio dealers
13 Ministry of Agriculture & Fisheries	13 Boulton-Seymour, ladies' hairdressers
15 Eye Edwin Chas confectioner	15 Dennis E. & Son, pork butchers
17 Hall Mrs. Freda, milliner	17 Flaire, curtain material dealer
19 Murdins Ltd office equipment **& School of Commerce**	19 Murdins Typewriter Co Ltd office equipment
21 Sayer Mrs F G tobacconist	21 Loveday E & V tobacconists
23 Bridge Hy newsagent	23 Bridge M E newsagent
25 Ward Jn. Douglas, greengrocer	25 Ward Douglas J. greengrocer
27	27
29 Bears Corn Stores, corn merchants	29 Wheelers (television dealers)
31	31 Wheelers (television dealers)
here is Tower Sreet	**here is Tower Sreet**
33 Building Material Co. Ltd	33 Ruymp Limited, builders' merchants
35 Building Material Co. Ltd	35 Ruymp Limited, builders' merchants
37 Building Material Co. Ltd	37 Ruymp Limited, builders' merchants
39 Pickett Mrs. MAE confectioner	39 Ruymp Limited, builders' merchants
41 Beaty's, florists	41 Hall LL Ltd (fancy goods dealers)
43 Gooding Stanley, hairdresser	43 John Anthony, hairdresser
45 Dobson Mrs. Norah, confectioner	45 Dobson Mrs. Norah, confectioner
47 Studio John Norman, photographers	47 Studio John Norman, photographers
49 St. James' Snack Bar	49 Cadenza, restaurant
51 St. James' Snack Bar	51 Jones Harold, wallpaper merchants
53 Shaw Mrs K A tobacconist	53 Central Newsagency
55 Tower Café	55 Bayes TV Ltd, electrical appliance retailers & television
here is Regent Place	**here is Regent Place**
59 Scaife E (house furnisher)	59 Norfolk County Constabulary Divisional Headquarters
here are St. James' & London Roads	**here are St. James' & London Roads**

TOP: The Youth Club was established in the early 1950s in Tower Street. The building had originally been a Wesleyan Methodist school hall, built in 1882. In the early 1950s it became the King's Lynn Youth Club.
The Youth Club was a great place for teenagers to meet. There were so many activities and anyone who was privileged to be associated with the club remembers it fondly as part of their happy formative years.
The pictures here and on the next page were all taken between the late 1950s and the late 1960s.

ABOVE: The cast of a play (circa 1961) who won a cup for the best performance in a county competition.

LEFT: The ticket for a dance in 1962 featuring Wee Willie Harris .

TOP: A Christmas party c1956.

MIDDLE LEFT: Performers in the club's Christmas Variety Show c1961.

RIGHT: A group from the Youth Club take a break at a transport café on the way to Luton airport before flying to Lloret de Mar (Spain) in 1967.
From left: Tony Tovell (Youth Leader), Sally Tovell, Ken Burgess, Lynn Starling, John Church, Henry Souttar, Chuck Hewitt, Richard Eke, Mary McLellan, Richard Booth, Joy McLellan, Carol Foreman, Martin Shirley, Maureen Dent, Peter Wadham, Chris Owen, John Darrington.

LEFT: Church Street in the late 1960s. On the right of the photo is JJ Eastick & Sons Ltd (radi wholesalers). Next door is the Workers Club. Further down is the Cosy Café.

BELOW: The staff of Eastick's in 1956. *Left to right*: John McDermid, John Croot, Norman Hastings, Stan Powles, Fred Smith and Joe Pegg

BOTTOM LEFT: Another view of Church Street in the late 60s.

BOTTOM RIGHT: Church Street at the junction with Priory Lane.

TOP: Blackfriars Street in the mid 60s. Judging by the assortment of bikes and prams, Miles Son & Landles are conducting an auction in the Blackfriars Hall. Just beyond is Juby & Co. (electricians).

ABOVE: Further down Blackfriars Street in 1959. The garages of Giles Bros and Philip H Johnson are clearly seen. Just beyond is Miss Evelyn Dye's (confectioner).

TOP: High Street on 20th July 1960. The properties beyond Jermyn's (Nos.5 to 9 High Street) are being demolished. Names lost to the street were GM Hartley (ladies & children's outfitters and drapers), Cheshire Cheese pub and Easters (radio & television).
ABOVE: Union Lane in 1959. This lane ran from beside Jermyn's (16 High Street) to 14 Tower Street. This photo was taken about halfway down the lane, looking towards High Street. The rear of the Majestic cinema is on the extreme right. Both ends of this lane are still intact today.

It's a Tuesday on the Cattle Market in August 1960.

TOP LEFT: There is a poultry auction taking place. TOP RIGHT: A general view of the cattle trucks. In the background can be seen the Museum.

ABOVE LEFT: The pig pens.

ABOVE RIGHT: This edge of the market (in 1963) is Albion Street and leads to Railway Road. The Stanley Arms pub sign can be seen - this pub was on the corner of Albion Street and Railway Road. The last livestock sale was on 28th June 1971.

ABOVE: Wisbech Road. The iron bridge (which had opened in 1886) over the River Nar, with the Gasworks on the right of the picture - taken c1960. The road sign indicating the approach to the South Gates roundabout is just beyond the bridge.

RIGHT:
The South Gates roundabout on 22nd June 1962.

BELOW LEFT:
Another view of South Gates roundabout with the Gasworks in the background c1960.

BELOW:
Lynn News picture from the front page of 10th July 1962 announcing the closure of the Gasworks. It was dismantled in 1964 Up to the 1960s our gas was produced here from coal (known as town gas). From then on the gas came from the North Sea (natural gas).

TOP LEFT: The main dock gate in May 1961. This was in St Ann's Fort (locally known as The Fort). The Fort was built in the 16th century in case the Spanish invaded from Holland. There was no defensive wall or ramparts - just sandbags. By the 18th century artillery was installed since there was a fear that the French might invade. If invasion was to come a sort of early 'Dad's Army' would be deployed!

TOP RIGHT: North Street in 1961 (looking from The Fort towards Pilot Street). The demolition was a result of the Town Council's clearance order of 1958. The North End Society at the time fought hard to stop this part of our fishing heritage being swept away. But like other important parts of our town, it disappeared.

ABOVE LEFT: A view of the desolation in North Street, from Pilot Street.

ABOVE RIGHT: Looking from Pilot Street to the corner of North Street we have, instead, a new garage - not exactly what the fishing community really needed!

As seen in the Lynn News in 1958
CLOCKWISE FROM TOP LEFT:
Announcement of the closure of the 'M&GN', a new pathology lab at the hospital, a new loco shed at South Lynn (perversely part of the closing M&GN!) - this new shed was opened in 1959, the same year the line closed. The 'Campbells are coming', the skiffle craze enjoys brief popularity and demolition in North End.

TOP: A view of the Dock Hotel on the corner of North Street and The Fort in the 1960s. The Dock Hotel closed after 150 years, in November 1961. It was the only pub with special licensing hours for the docks - it opened an extra ½ hour every week day afternoon. It was stated that the brewery planned to rebuild the Fisherman's Return (which was between the Pilot cinema and the dock railway line) and enlarge the Naval Reserve (seen at the rear of the parked van).

ABOVE: A view looking down St Ann's Street from The Fort. The Naval Reserve can be clearly seen, along with Harry Southgate's. The tall building in front of St Nicholas' spire is Humphrey's (ship chandlers). The empty corner of the street now forms the entrance to True's Yard.

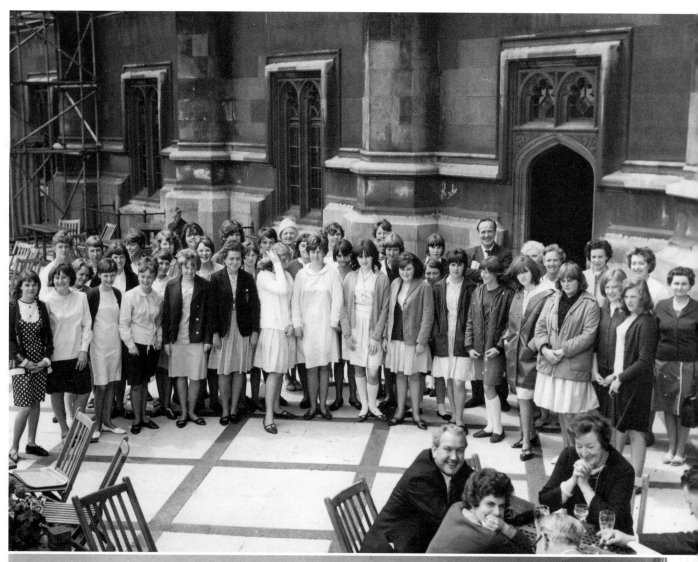

TOP: Gaywood Park Girls visit the House of Commons in 1961.

ABOVE: A harvest festival at Gaywood Park Girls school in 1964.

TOP: Looking down Railway Road from Stevens' corner in 1960. The Hunstanton bus (service 35) has stopped to pick up a passenger.

ABOVE: On the same day a view from the other side of the road. The garage of Bird and Varney is prominent. Sandwiched between the two parts of the garage is C&V Popkiss (upholsterers and cabinet makers). Two 'Tec' boys walk past the premises of AF Foreman & Sons (builders and contractors).

BAKER LANE.
From 103 High st. to 14 Queen st.
South side.
3a, Harral Jn
3 Greeves T. J. & Son, smiths
Dennick J. Herbert & Sons Ltd.
fertilizer mers. (garage)
4 Ringwood Leslie

North side.
Hallack & Bond (Wholesale)
Ltd. who. grocers
Bowker A. & J. maltsters (malt-
ings)

TOP: Baker Lane looking from Queen Street to High Street in August 1961.
ABOVE LEFT: Baker Lane from High Street looking to Queen Street in September 1961.
MIDDLE RIGHT: Baker Lane, Kelly's entry for 1960.
ABOVE RIGHT: High Street circa late 1960s. The pleasing Tudor style frontage of Broughton's (No.104) has been demolished and
replaced by a new featureless shop (Scotch Wool Shop).

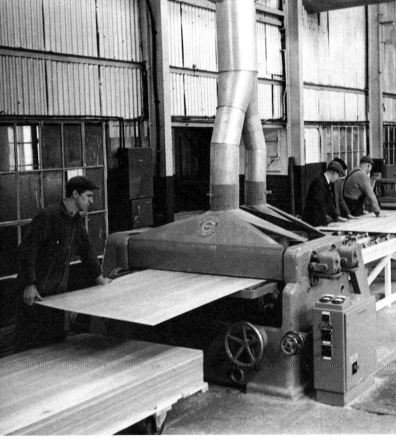

Timber was one of the Lynn's main imports (via the docks).

TOP: In 1961 the drivers of Pattrick & Thompson pose in the yard for the cameraman before setting off on their delivery rounds.
Left to right: Bill Wagg, Toby Jaggs, Jack Asker, ?, Bill Collison.

MIDDLE RIGHT: A view of Bristow & Copley's yard on the Bentinck dock.

ABOVE: The staff of Stanton's cut timber to order sometime in the 1960s.

BOTTOM RIGHT: Pattrick & Thompson's yard on the corner of the Alexandra Dock in the late 1950s.

Surrey Street runs from 11 Chapel Street to 64 High Street & 1 Tuesday Market Place.

TOP: Looking down the street (in 1962) to Jones & Dunn (outfitters) on the corner of High Street and Tuesday Market Place.

ABOVE LEFT: Lloyds Bank in 1962, on the corner of Surrey Street of the Tuesday Market.

RIGHT: Looking down Surrey Street (1962) towards Chapel Street.
The hanging sign of RH Setchell can be seen above their offices.
The cobbled street was mainly occupied by three firms. These were John Skinner & Sons (iron & metal merchants and sack & bag merchants),
RH Setchell & Sons Ltd (wholesale food distributors, fruit & vegetables, grocers, confectionery) and WJ Everitt (rag, metal & skin merchants).
In warm weather the pungent smell of the hanging animal pelts would fill the whole street!

TOP: A fashion show at Alderman Catleugh in the early 1960s.
Back row (left to right); ?, Diane Keen, Gill Manning, Carol Stimpson, Vanessa Graham, Susan Churchman, Janet Boon, ?, Lauren Edgley.
Front row: Vivienne Deacon, Linda Thompson, June Lemon, Maureen Goodbody, Lynda Brett, Gillian Wheatley, Janet Tingle, ?.

ABOVE: St Margaret's and St Faith's churches bell ringers outing, Whit Monday 1962. The photograph was taken on the market place in Kettering. Behind the bus is the Cherry Tree pub (dating back to 1695) and a newsagents called (co-incidentally) Linnetts.
Front row, kneeling: Miriam Higdon, Sonia Snasdell, Elizabeth Ward, Shirley Andrews, Diane Bowman, Wendy Twite.

TOP: Wisbech Road at the point where the harbour branch line crossed it in the mid 1960s. The pub in the middle of the picture is the Railway Tavern and was located between the railway and the Nar bridge (see top of page 58). Just to the left of the photographer and out of view is the entrance to Diamond Street and Winfarthing Avenue.
Behind the photographer the Wisbech Road and Saddlebow Road diverge.
ABOVE: Between 125 and 169 Saddlebow Road is the West Norfolk Fertilisers (already covered in 'Looking Back at Lynn'), but here can be seen the offices and laboratories on 17th January 1962. These two front buildings had only recently been built.
The huge building in the background housed the main 'compound' facility and phosphoric acid plant (used to make triple superphosphate fertilizer).

TOP: Inside the Post Office (Baxter's Plain) in November 1962. The mayor (Alderman Fred Jackson) is one of the first customers to buy a new issue of National Savings certificates. He is being served by Ray Bullock. Behind Mr Bullock is Mr C Williams (Head Postmaster) and Mr M Dyble (Assistant Head - extreme right). The man with grey hair watching the transaction is the prominent hospital surgeon, Mr Lewin. The other counter clerk is Douglas Ebbs and behind him is counter overseer Mr E Holford.

ABOVE: Miss GPO Personality Competition 1962.
Left to right: Maureen Cassidy, Daphne Wicks, Wendy Porter, Christine Proctor, Diane Baker, Wendy Vincent, Jane Barrett and Phyllis Orr.

TOP: A view of Gaywood Clock from Gayton Road in May 1961. The shop behind the Clock is a branch of King's Lynn Co-operative Society (KLCS) now being advertised as a self-service store. This is the last address in Lynn Road (No.83). To the right is the Cock Inn (No.1 Wootton Road). On the left of the picture a hanging sign advertises the Swan public house (No.4 Gayton Road).

ABOVE: Gaywood railway crossing taken from Gaywood Road in May 1961. The other side of the railway is Lynn Road. The line gates were replaced with a barrier in November 1961.

INSET: The clock nearing completion in 1925.

ABOVE: Austin Street looking east in May 1962. Behind the car the sun streams down Hope Yard and Railway Passage - the shop on the corner of the passage has long since closed. The tall building is the Co-op grocery ware-house. The roof just visible behind the Mann Egerton hoarding is part of the Co-op bakery and model dairy.

BOTTOM LEFT: Hope Yard in April 1962. To the left of this picture is now John Kennedy Road. At the bottom of he yard to the right of the alley can be seen a white building which can be seen today from John Kennedy Road (opposite Lidl's).

BOTTOM RIGHT: Railway Passage in April 1962. It is a few feet east of Hope Yard. This would be somewhere near the middle of oday's John Kennedy Road.

TOP: This quay was known as Paul's Mill or Friars Fleet (part of the Nar) and was adjacent to the Boal Quay. The picture was taken on Sunday 22nd April 1962. The Anno of Aberdeen had arrived from Rotterdam on the evening tide on the Friday with a cargo of 300 tons of grain. The quay is dominated by the mill of R&W Paul Ltd (animal food manufacturers).
This is only the second time this ship (built in Aberdeen in 1952) visited Lynn - the first time was in 1956 with a cargo of beet pulp.

ABOVE: Just to the left of the top picture is the swing bridge over the Nar which carried the Harbour Branch railway. This bridge had been built in 1855 - an identical one to the one over the Millfleet. These bridges were favourite short cuts to South Lynn - note the people on the left of the photo. Both bridges were removed using oxy-acetylene cutting equipment in early 1970.

ABOVE: May 1961. Townsend's Corner, named after Charles Townsend (corn merchants) which stood on the corner of Railway Road and Norfolk Street - from behind the bus stop down to the corner. Straight ahead to the right of Andrews shop front is entrance to Railway Passage (above the passage entrance is the number 92).

LEFT: A queue waits for a bus (Townsend's premises behind). This was probably the stop where most people would catch the bus for home. The main services picking up passengers here were for South Wootton, Gaywood Park, Newlyn and Hunstanton.

BELOW: 1962. Further up Railway Road, looking towards Townsend's Corner, two men take the low carbon option to transport their goods! The corner of Albion Street can be seen - the Stanley Arms clearly visible.

TOP RIGHT: No.30 Norfolk Street c1962, J & K Watson (tobacconists) is up for sale.
By the following year it had changed hands to become Heath & Heather Ltd (herbalists).

ABOVE: 20 years earlier (in 1942) the shop - under different ownership - was badly damaged when, on June 12th at 9.30 pm, a German Dornier bomber dropped several bombs on the town. The Eagle Hotel opposite the shop received a direct hit killing 42 local people and airmen billeted at the rear of the hotel. Another bomb landed i the cattle market behind Norfolk Street while two more bombs hit the Walks (between the Wood Street council depot and the Re Mount). The Eagle had to be completely demolished.

BELOW: In 1960 a man walks past the new Eagle Hotel which had been opened in September 1959. Just beyond the Eagle reconstruction of the rest of the bombed site is taking place. This was to become the Elmo supermarket. Opposite can be seen th 'Capstan' sign of the tobacconists.

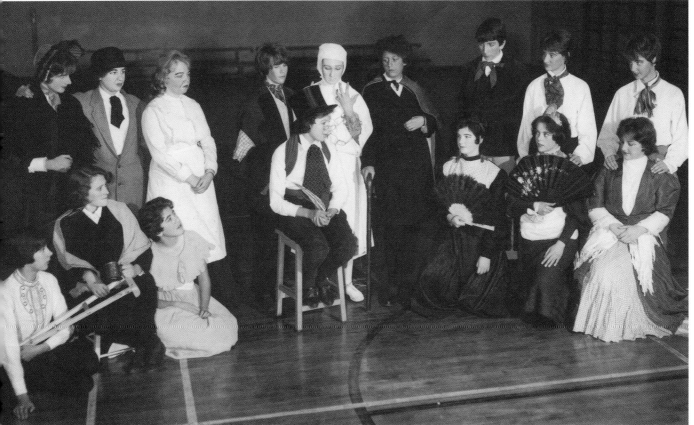

TOP: Alderman Catleugh girls visit the Houses of Parliament in 1963. Later that day the group went to see Tommy Steele in Half a Sixpence.

ABOVE: 'A Christmas Carol' by Charles Dickens is performed by the Alderman Catleugh Girls in December 1961.
Back row: Rosemary Cousins, Susan Wright, June Smith, Diane Malcolm, Carol Stimpson, Christine Wilmore, Angela Reynolds, Nanette Lock, Linda Thompson.
Front row: Jenny Christmas, Wendy Chadwick, Maureen Rudd, Sue Mansell, Janet Lusher, Janet Bone, Ruby Rust.

ABOVE: High Street in 1965. I cropped this picture to make the cover of the last book but have had requests to see what the full picture looked like without the titles!

RIGHT: The girls of Ladymans looking down on the street in 1949 catch the eye of an EDP cameraman. They are Daphne Worrell, Margaret Worrell, Lucy Hudson and Beryl Tann.

BOTTOM RIGHT: May 1962 outside Ladyman's. Just employed by the company, Pat Lemon has been assigned her first job - literally starting on the bottom rung of the ladder! The Lynn News, quick to spot a story, printed this picture describing her as Lynn's first 'teenage ladder minder'.

TOP: Norfolk Street in 1963. The place to buy the latest mens fashion was Barrons. The business had been started by Peter Dunham in the early 1950s at 140, Norfolk Street, and had previously been RJ Brooke (china dealer).

ABOVE: Looking in the opposite direction in 1961 towards Woolworths. The shop on the right is R&A Taylor Ltd (seed & bulb merchants) - in this year the firm had been trading on this site for 106 years. The Coffee House [3, Norfolk Street is TR Wagg (bakers)] and the acquired property was Ely's (bakers) at No.4 and Barnett & Hutton at No.5 (costumiers) - this had been Metcalf & Spreckley (chemists) until the mid 1950s. On the extreme left of the picture is White Lion Court, which is still evident today.

TOP: Lynn Pub licensees' ladies night at the Town Hall in the mid 1960s.

MIDDLE RIGHT: 'You can lead a horse to water……..' The Rummer (mid 1960s). Landlord Jack Cherrington gives a horse a drink, watched by landlady Betty Cherrington. I remember a stool in the bar that had been signed by Arth Haynes - is that him in the background?

MIDDLE LEFT: The Rummer (on the corner of Tower Street and St James Street). Behind the bar are Jack & Betty, while Betty's brother (left) serves TV personality Diana Coupland.

LEFT: The bar of the Captain Vancouver (Gaywood Park). On the left is landlord Harry Lusher and third from left is Kath Manning-Coe.

TOP: Littleport Street in 1958, looking towards the Hob in the Well. All the properties that stood along here to Littleport Terrace (including Cross Yard) have, by now, disappeared.

ABOVE: Looking in the opposite direction in January 1963, the only properties which survived along this side of the street were The Duke of Edinburgh pub (on the corner of Blackfriars Road) and Nos. 4 ("Danum") & 6 ("Silverwood") Littleport Street. Lynn Service Station had been built in 1962. Behind this site is St James Primary Girls'/Infants' school. The turning into Littleport Terrace is in the left foreground.

Sedgeford Lane in 1963, looking from Tower Street. Out of view on the left is the Majestic cinema (built in 1928).

The pub (The Foresters Arms), built in 1901, closed in August 1969. This pub had no licence to sell spirits and could only sell beer. The other end of lane ran from 26, High Street and that end still has its street sign in place.

ABOVE: King's Lynn station on 3rd May 1969. The last day of service for the Hunstanton line. Enthusiasts pay their last respects, photograph and ride on the trains on this day. The line had opened on 3rd October 1866. Unfortunately the government wanted to spend vast amounts of money on roads at the expense of the railways. Bearing in mind the increasing traffic congestion on the roads, this may prove to have been a short sighted view.

BELOW: A sand train is arriving from Middleton Towers (the Norwich line). Two sets of sidings can be seen in the background. The sidings to the right (Exton's Road sidings) held goods wagons, while the sidings on the Norwich line held coaching stock. These sidings were known as California sidings. The derivation of the name is thought to come from the wartime when coaching stock stored here was used to ferry American forces. This line to Swaffham and East Dereham was closed on 7th September 1968. East Dereham to Wymondham closed a year later but remained open for freight for a further twenty years. Only the section to Middleton currently exists for the transportation of sand.

BELOW RIGHT: Tramps & Vamps Ball at the Red Cat (North Wootton) in 1965.
Left to right: Derek Chappell, Jill Fitzhugh, Diana Priddle, Linda Francis, Graham Thomson, Joan Thomson, Myra Grant.

TOP LEFT: In 1963 David Andrews receives the Baden Powell award from Assistant District Commissioner Charlie Bew. Looking on from the left: David Birdseye, Terry Krill, Bill Dick, Gordon Terrey, Jack Whomes & Ian Savage.
TOP RIGHT: Ingoldisthorpe Manor September 1964. Mr Thornhill (retiring manager of the Midland Bank) and his wife receive gifts from the staff.
BELOW LEFT: Members of The Fur & Feather Club in 1954.

TOP: Page Stair Lane in 1962. The lane runs from 17, Tuesday Market Place.
ABOVE: Page Stair Lane looking toward the Tuesday Market Place. The property to the right belongs to Whiteley & Creasy Ltd (caravan distributors). The building in the middle of the picture is the Lynn Laundry Ltd. Behind the photographer is the river.

TOP: The North Star pub in Lady Jane Grey Road (North Lynn) in January 1964. The pub has recently been demolished to make way for flats.

ABOVE: The Co-op (or King's Lynn & District Working Men's Co-Operative Society Ltd) at Seabank, North Lynn in 1963. Besides being a grocery shop it was also a post office. Like many post offices this is now closed. At the time the photograph was taken the Post Office Service (which incorporated the telephone system) was a profitable business. As well as this one, there were post offices in Lynn at Alexandra Dock (St Ann's Fort), All Saint's Street, Eastgates (96, Norfolk Street), Gaywood (3, Wootton Road), North End (7, Loke Road), South Lynn (57, London Road), Tennyson Avenue, West Lynn, Wisbech Road, Mill Lane and the main post office on Baxter's Plain. Unfortunately the various services have been stripped out (starting with the formation of BT) leaving a business struggling to survive.

Five more groups in our 'beat' contest

IN the second part of our swinging contest to find West Norfolk's top "beat" group, which we introduced last week, we publish below the second list of groups.

The top group is something you — the fans — must decide and soon there will be a voting form published in "The Young Set" to enable you to send in your first three choices for top group and top vocalist.

The "Lynn News and Adviser" and Messrs. Bayes, the Lynn record shop, are holding the contest to encourage up-and-coming young musicians and singers.

Offbeats

PERHAPS the best known group in the area — and certainly the oldest — The Offbeats, have recently cut four records for the Decca recording company.

Formed six years ago, they began playing at the Kit Kat, Hunstanton, shortly after the skiffle boom ended.

Based originally on the...

...booked for dance hall dates.

Within four months they were playing at Norwich, Lynn, Wisbech and Cambridge...

THE FULL LIST

SO that you know who the groups are in the area, here is a list of them, and the singers who you can vote for.

GROUPS: The Pagans; The Valiants; The Hitch Hikers; The Megatons; The Coasters; The Zodiacs; The Electrons; The Panthers; Group X; The Devil's Coachmen; The Strollers; Lombard and the Tea Time Four; The Trojans; The Offbeats; The Sabres; The Escorts; The Countdowns; Johnny and the Coasters; any other group.

SINGERS: Danny Ford (The Offbeats); Danny Eves (The Strollers); Mike Prior (The Escorts); Denny Raven (The Sabres); Larry Bond (The Trojans); Tony Cator (The Zodiacs); Tony Batterbee (The Valiants); Dick Woods (Lombard and the Tea Time Four); Dave Reed (The Pagans), Terry Rose (Devil's Coachmen); Keith Steele (Hitch Hikers); any other vocalists.

Members of the group are Graham Williamson — drums, Rodney Shirley — bass guitar, Michael Williamson — lead guitar and Larry Bond — vocalist.

MARIE BEESTON (15) holds the trophies which can be won by the "beat" group and singer voted into the top position in our competition. Marie works for Messrs. Bayes record shop, who are providing these challenge trophies. (GC.2637).

Five more groups in our 'beat' contest

IN the second part of our swinging contest to find West Norfolk's top "beat" group, which we introduced last week, we publish below the second list of groups.

THE Tea Time Four, winners of the Top Beat Group competition. Left to right: John Cork, Raymond Burrell (Baz), Brian Brown (Rocky), Mike Prior (vocalist winner), Bernard Rudd (Berny) and Barry Dean (Fats). (GC 3189).

Tea Time Four & Mike Prior win the challenge trophies

HERE it is ... the result of our Top Beat Group and Top Vocalist competition. Readers sent in 2,140 entries and the result judged on the popular vote was:

	TOP GROUP	
1	TEA TIME FOUR	774
2	THE SABRES	587
3	THE OFFBEATS	450
	TOP VOCALIST	
1	MIKE PRIOR (Tea Time Four)	649
2	DENNY RAVEN (Sabres)	494
3	DANNY FORD (Offbeats)	455

TOP LEFT: The Devil's Coachmen. *Left to right* [Brian (Dacious) Cook, Terry Rose, Michael (Buggy) Wilson and Chris Ashby].

MIDDLE RIGHT: The Offbeats at the Kit Kat in 1964. The place to go on Sunday nights in the 60s was the Kit Kat, where the top band was the Offbeats (who played upstairs) while a guest band played downstairs. *Left to right*: Nick Carter, Danny Ford, Derek Stringer, Tony Pull and Nigel Portass. The Offbeats were the first of the bands to form in 1958.

ABOVE LEFT: The Escorts in 1962. *Left to right* (Pete Carter, Rick Meek, Mike Prior and Alan Drake). The Lynn News cuttings refer to the 1964 'Beat Group' competition to find the most popular local group. The winners (Tea Time Four) received cups for best group and best singer (Mike Prior) plus a recording session in Bayes recording studio in Tower Street.

TOP: Norfolk Street at the junction with Railway Road in 1964. Part of the Co-op, Andrew's (Chemists), Mrs Ashwood's hairdressers and KH East & Co Ltd (rope manufacturers) have disappeared in the preparation of the new John Kennedy Road.
ABOVE: The other end of Railway Road at the junction with Blackfriars Street and St James Road - known as Stevens' Corner [after Samuel Stevens (fishmonger), who occupied the shop on the corner in the early part of the 20th century].

ABOVE: Blackfriars Road in 1965, looking toward the corner with Norfolk Street. The sign 'Hire C.F.& G advertises the sack hire depot of Chisholm, Fox & Garner Ltd. This and the adjoining property had been a blacksmiths (run by the Thrower family) and a carting contractors (run by the Lubbock family). Both these businesses had been in existence for over fifty years.

RIGHT: A view looking down Coburg Street from Blackfriars Road in the mid 1960s. This is Lower Canada - the proposal to clear the area was made in 1961 about 100 years after it had been built.

BELOW: 1966. My house and the rest of Lower Canada has gone another community obliterated from the map of Lynn. They may be able to knock our homes down but they can't take away our happy memories - watching trains from my attic bedroom window, my first chemistry experiments in the coalhouse making gunpowder…...

TOP: London Road in the mid 1960s. Someone is learning to drive the milk float. The shop on the extreme left is Fullers Radio & Television Ltd (No.124 London Road). There are no traffic lights at the junction with the Millfleet. Possibly the only traffic lights i Lynn at this time were the Townsend's Corner lights.

ABOVE: Another view from the other side of the road. The gap between Fullers and the house (No.125) was built on within the nex year or two to become DF Booth (turf accountant) and the empty shop became Eric's (hardware merchants). RF Bennett (newsagen occupies Nos. 128 & 129, while the house with the wall round was Lister Hammond (cycles) but had ceased trading.

TOP: Tower Street in 1966. The Phoenix becomes one of the first Chinese restaurants in town. To the left of the picture is FA Stone (tobacconist and sweet shop). I wonder how the PC lobby would feel about children going in to a sweet shop with the strong aroma of tobacco! As teenagers we used to try all the exotic cigarettes. I remember Black Sobrani (Russian I think), they looked really cool as they were black with a gold filter. The archway to the right is Leach's Yard. Harry Brien ran his French polishing business here. Harry was also a great pub pianist and a colourful character to boot.

ABOVE: Tower Street in 1962. The man on the ladder in South Clough Lane might be in for a shock as the van appears to be about to turn right down the lane! Next to Peter Loades is the popular Jimmy & Jean Dawson's Book & Toy Shop.

TOP: In 1967 the King's Lynn Operatic & Dramatic Society (KLODS) put on The Merry Widow at the Theatre Royal. At the front of the ensemble is Angela Rose singing in the title role.

ABOVE: 1967. King's Lynn Sea Cadet Corps. The photograph was taken at the TS (training ship) Vancouver on the South Quay. There was also a girls group (Girls Nautical Training Corps or GNTC) who met in a hut in Loke Road near the Gaywood river. Not too long after this picture was taken the two amalgamated and now all meet at the TS Vancouver.

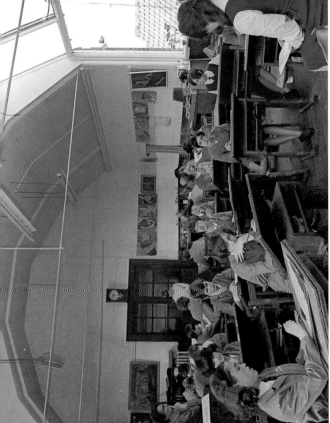

The High School (more correctly (West Norfolk & King's Lynn High School for Girls) in 1967.

TOP RIGHT:
An Art class in progress.

TOP FAR RIGHT:
The front of the school from King Street early in the morning.

BOTTOM RIGHT:
In the courtyard.

BOTTOM FAR RIGHT:
The rear of the school. The school had the best rear aspect of any school in Lynn - a beautiful lawned garden with a view of the river.

Taylor's Garage, Broad Street in 1967. This was originally The Electric Theatre and was built in 1911. The last film shown in April 1938 was 'The Bad Guy'. I believe this was the first cinema to hold 'Saturday morning pictures' for children. After the war the Pilot carried on this tradition for a short time until the Majestic* took over in 1948.

During the war it was used as an army barracks, and after the war became Taylor's Garage (which had been established elsewhere in 1933). The façade, by this time, had been much altered although the upper part including the balustrade remained until the building was demolished in 1969 to make way for the poor architecture that was the Vancouver Centre.

* Who remembers the sing-song before the films: "We are the boys and girls well known as the minors of the ABC….."?

TOP: Windsor Road in the late 1960s. On the left is Pauline Hair Stylist (on the corner of Pleasant Row)), next door is SH Petts (confectioner) and SH Petts (grocers).

RIGHT: The Ordnance Survey map shows the layout of the streets in this community (just above the top of the map is London Road).

All this is about to be swept away - by the end of the 60s all the properties had been demolished.

MIDDLE LEFT: Keppel Street looking towards Windsor Road.

BOTTOM LEFT: The house on the right of the picture has been vacated while the other two houses still appear to be lived in.

93

TOP: The Millfleet in early 1967. A man draws on his cigarette and contemplates the changes about to take place.

In May 1967 the bulldozers moved in to demolish another community. This time it was the turn of Coronation Square, Providence Street, Union Street, Chadwick Street, Vicarage Lane and Hillington Square (after which the whole new development would be named). ABOVE: By January 1968 the old was being replaced by the new. Was the old community spirit going to carry forward to the new?

TOP: The corner of Union Street and All Saints Street in October 1966. The large house behind the bonfire is Welwick House. This was originally a museum and, in the 1950s, it was the home of King's Lynn Society of Arts & Sciences. Although a listed building it still had to go to make way for the new Hillington Square development.

ABOVE: A view of the Millfleet taken from Providence Street. St Margaret's School can be seen with the Greyfriars Tower behind. The street in the bottom right-hand corner of the picture is Chadwick Street while the track from the middle left of the picture is all that is left of Vicarage Lane.

TOP LEFT & RIGHT: New Conduit Street in the late 1960s. It wouldn't be long before the bulldozers moved in here.

LEFT: The Empire cinema (built in 1913) lasted only 55 years but had to go - the two men probably remembering the good times they had here as lads, at the 'silent pictures'!

BELOW: Tower Street in March 1968. Nos.15 to 19 were being demolished to make way for the new East Anglian Trustee Savings Bank who were moving from High Street. This had been Dees of King's Lynn (florists and fruiterers).

ABOVE: The late 1960s and more demolition - this time the Grosvenor and Fiddaman's are the victims. This is part of the Broad Street development (to be named the Vancouver Centre). Today it is now called the Vancouver Quarter!

At this time cars can travel freely down both Norfolk Street and Broad Street - this was soon to be pedestrianised.

RIGHT: This photograph has been taken from the almost identical spot. It is a cold, bleak January morning in 1952.

The Grosvenor is on the right of the picture while a hanging sign advertises Turner's Hairdressing Saloon (not the more elegant term 'salon' adopted by modern hairdressers).

The next property along is the Chain Lending Library. The road to the left is Chapel Street and beyond that is The Flower Pot public house. Almost opposite Chapel Street is Broad Street.

Cooper's Roller Bearings is renowned throughout the world. Thomas Cooper was already known for his inventions and innovations when he opened his new works on Wisbech Road in 1894. Originally he built steam diggers, cars and bombs (used in the 1914-18 war). In the 1920s roller bearings became the main focus of production, culminating in the Cooper split roller bearing - far superior to any rivals.

TOP: An aerial view of the works in 1951. In the background is South Lynn railway sidings.

MIDDLE LEFT: Women working in the machine shop c1944 making vital bearings needed for artillery, searchlights and propeller shafts for ships.

MIDDLE RIGHT: A view of the works from Wisbech Road. The tall structure (or twin cupolas) was part of a furnace for melting metals - later replaced by an electric furnace.

BOTTOM LEFT: Casting molten metal in the ferrous (iron) foundry in the early 1960s.

In the late 1950s the new Jodrell Bank radio telescope was fitted with large Cooper split roller bearings. The company continues to thrive today and is one of our town's success stories.

In 1960 the town boasted very many family run businesses and although the premises were, in many cases, very small they offered a fair range of products. There was no mass migration of foods from across the world in order to satisfy having, say, strawberries or sweet tomatoes every day. The waiting for the seasonal product made it taste that much better. Do we really need exotic foods from thousands of miles away - at a serious cost to the planet? Here is a list of some shops (most of which have gone), but the names will be familiar to our generation. This is my tribute to all those who gave us service and more importantly their time and consideration to make a modest living in fulfilling our needs.

GROCERS

Begley CA 8 Front Row, Highgate
Booth WL & Sons, 91 Wootton road
Culey Jn W 40A, Hillen road
Corner Stores (The) 7 Loke road
Daynes GE & Son, 60 London road
Edwards Mrs VMA 14 Wootton road
Ferlisi Mrs LK 25 Blackfriars road
Fillenham's Variety Stores
25 Wootton road
Francis Mrs L 3 Valinger's road
Frost's Stores, 31 Providence street
Gower R & W 17/19 Windsor road
Greenhalgh R 154 St Peter's road
W Lynn
Hannam & Barnard, 31 Tennyson
avenue
Hare Mrs K 181 St Peter's road
West Lynn
Holder Wm V 24 Wisbech road
Home & Colonial Stores 107 High street
Hutton Mrs M 10 Market street
International Stores Ltd. 103 High street
Iago Fredk 33 All Saints street
Jubey Mrs. DE 47 South Everard street
Ladyman JH Ltd, 39 to 41 High street
Laws GP 2 Oak circle
Lee Wltr South Wootton
Marsters Arth L 3 Wootton road
Maypole Dairy Co Ltd 39 High street
Melias Ltd 123 Norfolk street
Panks Percy W Rosebery avenue
Peckover CW. 15 Littleport street
Petts Stanley, 13 Windsor road
Ransom Herbt G North Wootton
Reed AE 1 Ferry sq. W Lynn &
12 Broad street
Self Victor M & Son, 7 St. James' road
Sidgwick H G 45/47 Wisbech road
Simpson Mrs V 9 Guanock terrace
Smith Bros 237 Saddlebow road
Smith SJT 46 Lansdowne street
Southgate S Ltd 1a, Losinga road
Southgate Hy D 7 St Ann's fort/
2 St Ann's street
Star Supply Stores, 37 High street
Thompson Mrs I 18 Albert street
Twite Albt G 25/26 Norfolk street
Wheatley Mrs Aline S 57 Chapel street

SHOPKEEPERS

Betts Mrs JS 9 Saturday Market Place
Bowdich PT 18 St. Nicholas street
Bowman Mrs DD 17 Loke road
Carter Mrs MJ 7 Lynn road
Causton W 13a, South Clough lane
Chase Ernest J 48 Loke road
Dawson SC 58 Lynn road
Dinage Mrs B 33 Birchwood street
Drew AJ Rilna stores, Castle Rising road
South Wootton
Elfleet F 39 Windsor road
Ess J Wm 2 St. James' place
Giles Wm Ernest, 30 Kitchener street
Groom Mrs W 10 Exton's place
Hodgson Gordon, 19 Church street
Hough JV 29 Church street
Lane Miss Lilian, 21 South Clough lane
Leverett Mrs MG 60 Loke road
Lilley C 70a, Norfolk street
Mitchell Mrs J 21 Checker street
Moore L. 47 Lynn road
Ramm WE & Son, 85 Saddlebow road
Ridout & Pearman, 19 Sir Lewis street
Royle FD 75 Friars street
Salmon WD 27 Wyatt street
Savage Wilfred Arth Hy 6 Exton's road
Sidgwick Mrs. Annie M. 4 Loke road
Smith & Thurston, 11 Chapel street
Sullivan Mrs F 23 Coronation square
Tann E & K 20 Millfleet
Thurston Herbt B 16 Cresswell street
Wilkinson & Hill, 281 Wootton road
Woodhead Stanley, 53 Railway road

RESTAURANTS & REFRESHMENT ROOMS

Broad Street Dining Rooms,
11 Broad street
Ely Wm & Sons, 4 Norfolk street (bakers)
Glendevon Hotel & Restaurant, 49/51
Railway road
Grosvenor (The), 13 Norfolk street
Jeep Restaurant (LL Hall), 2/3
Paradise parade
Ladyman JH & Co (The Gallery
Restaurant & Café & Snack Bar)
39 to 41 High street
Limberts Ltd. 109 Norfolk street

Lowe's Restaurant (Reynolds Ltd.),
3 Norfolk street
Thurston CA 341 Wootton road
Woodcock AB Ltd. 50 High street
& 116 Norfolk street (bakers)

CAFES/SNACK BARS

Alexander Mrs E Wisbech road
Bedford Cafe, Blackfriars road
Blackfriars Café, Blackfriars road
Cox E (The Pink Grill) 8 Tower street
Emlen Café (LL Hall, propr.), 41 St.
James' street
John Deen's Café, 77 Lynn road
Potter Mrs. Emily, 13 Queen street
Regal, 3 New Conduit street
Rowe Stanley, 17 & 18 Millfleet
Wimpy, 49 St. James street

BUTCHERS

Arrowsmith AW 1 All Saints street
Barber C. A. 49 Norfolk street
Baxters (Butchers) Ltd 35 & 122 High
street, 136 Norfolk street
Blomfield T W 54 London road
Bowers George, 8 St. James' street
Clarke Arth J 126 Norfolk street
Davy Miss G 38 Loke road
Dewhurst JH Ltd 2a, Norfolk street
Durrant Winston 87/89 Wootton road
G Eastmans Ltd. 1 Broad street
Fletcher W & B Ltd. 99a High street
Foreman R & Sons 32 Windsor road
Grummett Bros 2 Valinger's road
Howard F W 115 London road
Lock Chas B 17 Norfolk street
Mason Wilfred F 63/64 Norfolk street
Milton Wilfred A Baxter's plain
Neal Frank, 25 Wisbech road
Prior EH & Sons Ltd 164 St.Peter's
road West Lynn
Prior EH 6 Saturday Market place
Sampson Cyril S 1 Oak circle
Sawyer AG 30 St. James' street
Scupham Chas W & Son 103
Norfolk street
Thomas Mark Geo 105 Norfolk street
Willgress Rt 59 Friars street
Woollard 12 Chapel street

PORK BUTCHERS

Batterbee & Co. 20 Tower street
Bunting GE & TF 34 Windsor road
Dale Fredk & Son, 31 Purfleet street
Dennis E. & Son, 15 St. James' street, 21
Chapel street & 64 Lynn road
George HE & Sons Ltd. Church street
Lancaster Wm A 22 Tower street
Morley Herbt 56 Norfolk street
Van Pelt Mrs F 108 Norfolk street

Kershaw L & J 42 Norfolk st
Miles Wltr. H. Wisbech road
Misson A. 11 Loke road
Morley Ernest Geo. 27 Wisbech road
Russell Mrs K West Winch
Ryder & Crosskill, 14 Broad street
Waters Mrs. Ada, 50 Norfolk street
Westwood Misses, 6 St. James' street

TOBACCONISTS

Alexander SA (AH Browne), 45 Lynn
road
Ash Chas Fredk 57 Norfolk street
Bannister DW Baxter's plain
Fillenham's Variety Stores, 25 Wootton
road
Finlay & Co Ltd. 53 High street
Garner F 96 Norfolk street
Hill Miss Alice, 12 Tower street
Hornigold Mrs EM 32(Purfleet street
Langford & Fidment, 17 & 18 Blackfriars
road & 128 Norfolk street
London Kiosks Ltd 1 Norfolk street
Loveday E & V 21 St. James' street
Misson A 11 Loke road
Starling Mrs FI 40/42 Windsor road
Stone Miss Florence, 9 Tower street
Watson J & K 30 Norfolk street

CONFECTIONERS

Bonds, 14 Millfleet
Booth Mrs Florence M 26 Pilot street
Broom Rt J 42 Wisbech road
Bullen Miss Gertrude 4 Saturday
Market place
Bullen Mrs. I 2 London road
Cobbold L. Baxter's plain
Dobson Mrs. Norah, 45 St. James'
street
Dye Miss Evelyn Mary, 24 Blackfriars
street
East Misses C & A 52 Norfolk street
Elms Stanley, 3 Tower place
Fillenham's Variety Stores 25 Wootton
road
Harrington Mrs DA 11 Windsor road
Haylett Mrs D 50 London road
Heys Ltd. 4 High street
Higgleton Mrs. A 8 Wootton road
Hume Mrs. Winifred M 19 Millfleet
Jago Fredk. 12/14 Blackfriars street
Kerry L. W 27 London road

HOTELS

Bowling Green Inn, 68/70 Checker street
Cozens Hotel Ltd Blackfriars street
Duke's Head Hotel Tuesday Market place
East Anglian, Blackfriars road
Globe Hotel King street
Guanock, South gates
Station (Jn. B. Howe), 265 Saddlebow road
Stonegate Hotel, 1 Stonegate street
Wenn's Commercial Hotel, Saturday
Market place & 123 High street
Glendevon Hotel 49/51 Railway road

PUBS

Albert, 21 Albert street
Anchor Inn, 6 South Lynn plain
Barley Mow, 2 Railway road
Bentinck, 21 Loke road
Bird-in-Hand, 19 Norfolk street
Black Horse, 26 Chapel street
Captain Vancouver, Oak circle
Carpenters' Arms, 122/123 London road
Cattle Market Tavern, 24 Broad street
Chequers Inn, 7 Southgate street
Cherry Tree, 81 St. Peter's rd West Lynn
Cheshire Cheese, 8 High street
Clough Fleet Tavern, 72 Blackfriars street
Cock Inn, 1 Woptton road
Crossways, Valinger's road
Crown & Mitre, Ferry street
Crystal Palace, Railway road
Diamond Jubilee, 13 Lynn road
Discovery, Losinga road
Dock Hotel, 2 North street
Duke of Connaught, 2 St. Nicholas street
Duke of Edinburgh, Littleport street
Duke of Fife, 5 Saturday Market place
Eagle Hotel, Norfolk street
Engineers' Tavern, 1 Coburg street
Estuary Tavern, 5 Ferry sq. West Lynn
Fiddamans, 11 Norfolk street

Fisherman's Arms, 36 Pilot street
Fisherman's Return, 52 Pilot street
Flower Pot, 132 Norfolk street
Foresters Arms, 29 Sedgeford lane
Freebridge Hotel, 133 Clenchwarton road
West Lynn
Golden Ball, 4 Tower street
Greyfriars Tavern, Blackfriars road
Hob-in-the-Well, Littleport street
Honest Lawyer, 60a, London road
House on the Green, North Wootton
Hulk Inn, 38 Bridge street
Jolly Farmers, 38 Wisbech road
Lincoln Tavern, 13 Millfleet
Live & Let Live, 18 Windsor road

London Porter House, 78 London road
Lord Kelvin, 7/9 Market street
Lord Napier Inn, 1 Guanock terrace
Maid's Head Inn, 7 Tuesday Market place
Mariners' Arms, South quay
Mariners' Compass, 36 Providence street
Naval Reserve, 1 St. Ann's street
New Inn, 349 Wootton road
Norwich Arms, 104 Norfolk street
Portland Arms, Wisbech road
Prince of Wales Hotel, 6a, Southgates
Princess Royal, 1 Blackfriars street
Queen's Arms Inn, 15 London road
Queen's Head, 45 High street
Railway Hotel, Blackfriars road
Railway Tavern, Wisbech road
Rose & Thistle, 15 South Clough lane
Royal Standard, County Court road
Rummer, Tower street
Sandringham, 9 Littleport street
Seven Sisters, 3 Exton's road
Ship, 29 Lynn road
Sportsman, West Winch road
Spotted Cow, St. James' place
Spread Eagle, 19 Gaywood road
Stanley Arms, 14 Railway road
Swan, 4 Gayton road
Swan, South Wootton
Swan Inn, 107 St. Peter's road. West Lynn
Tilden Smith, 54 Pilot street
Victoria, Estuary road
Victory Inn, 12 Tuesday Market place
Volunteer Stores, 1 Union street
White Hart Stores, 1 St. James' street
White Horse, 7 Wootton road
Woolpack, 112/114 Gaywood road
Woolpack, 22 Tuesday Market place